SIMONE BILES

★ OLYMPIC GYMNAST ★

KATIE LAJINESS

Big Buddy Books
An Imprint of Abdo Publishing
abdopublishing.com

BIG BUDDY **OLYMPIC** BIOGRAPHIES

abdopublishing.com

Published by Abdo Publishing, a division of ABDO, PO Box 398166, Minneapolis, Minnesota 55439.
Copyright © 2017 by Abdo Consulting Group, Inc. International copyrights reserved in all countries.
No part of this book may be reproduced in any form without written permission from the publisher.
Big Buddy Books™ is a trademark and logo of Abdo Publishing.

Printed in the United States of America, North Mankato, Minnesota.
102016
012017

 THIS BOOK CONTAINS
RECYCLED MATERIALS

Cover Photo: epa european pressphoto agency b.v./Alamy Stock Photo
Interior Photos: AP Images for Kellogg's (p. 27); ASSOCIATED PRESS (pp. 5, 10, 17, 19, 25, 31);
    Cal Sport Media/Alamy Stock Photo (p. 15); epa european pressphoto agency b.v./Alamy
    Stock Photo (p. 17); Erich Schlegel/Alamy Stock Photo (p. 19); © IStockphoto.com (p. 13);
    ITAR-TASS Photo Agency/Alamy Stock Photo (p. 11); THOMAS COEX/Staff/Getty Images (p. 9);
    Tribune Content Agency LLC/Alamy Stock Photo (p. 23); ZUMA Press, Inc./Alamy Stock Photo
    (pp. 13, 21, 29).

Coordinating Series Editor: Tamara L. Britton
Graphic Design: Jenny Christensen

Publisher's Cataloging-in-Publication Data

Names: Lajiness, Katie, author.
Title: Simone Biles / by Katie Lajiness.
Description: Minneapolis, MN : Abdo Publishing, 2017. | Series: Big buddy
    Olympic biographies | Includes bibliographical references and index.
Identifiers: LCCN 2016953145 | ISBN 9781680785500 (lib. bdg.) |
    ISBN 9781680785784 (ebook)
Subjects: LCSH: Biles, Simone, 1997- --Juvenile literature. | Women gymnasts--
    United States--Biography--Juvenile literature. | Women Olympic athletes--
    United States--Biography--Juvenile literature. | Olympic Games (31st : 2016 :
    Rio de Janeiro, Brazil)
Classification: DDC 794.44/092 [B]--dc23
LC record available at http://lccn.loc.gov/2016953145

CONTENTS

OLYMPIC STAR

Simone Biles is a famous gymnast. In 2016, Simone won four gold **medals** at the Olympics. She has won more world titles than any other female gymnast in history. People consider Simone one of the greatest gymnasts of all time.

EARLY YEARS

Simone Arianne Biles was born in Columbus, Ohio, on March 14, 1997. Simone's mother was unable to care for Simone and her **siblings**. For a while, Simone spent time with other families in **foster homes**.

WHERE IN THE WORLD?

FAMILY TIES

In 1999, Simone and her younger sister Adria went to live with Ronald and Nellie Biles in Spring, Texas. When Simone was six, the couple adopted the two girls. They call Ronald and Nellie Mom and Dad.

DID YOU KNOW?

Nellie Biles is from Belize. So, Simone is a citizen of both the United States and Belize! Belize is a country in South America.

Ronald and Nellie Biles are Simone's grandparents. But, she considers them to be her parents.

STARTING OUT

As a child, Simone was always bouncing around and doing flips. At age six, she began gymnastics classes. Two years later, **coach** Aimee Boorman noticed Simone's talent. She began coaching Simone.

Simone and coach Aimee (*right*) are very close. Aimee knows when to give Simone a break. She also knows when to push Simone harder.

Simone was the first student Aimee coached to the Olympic level.

As Simone's talent grew, she spent most of her time at the gym. She trained hard and continued to learn new gymnastics skills. Simone **competed** and won many junior gymnastics events.

DID YOU KNOW?

In 2013, Simone became the first African-American all-around world champion.

In 2012, Simone was the US Secret Gymnastics Competition all-around champion.

Many gymnasts wear grips to protect their hands.

13

BIG DREAMS

Simone wanted to be the best gymnast in the world. She trained about 32 hours each week. **Coach** Aimee and Simone also made time for Simone to have fun outside the gym.

DID YOU KNOW?

Simone started homeschooling when she was 13. A tutor worked with her between gymnastics practices.

Sometimes, Simone had to make hard decisions in order to reach her dreams. She gave up many things to train for the Olympics.

ALL-AROUND SUPERSTAR

Simone continued to win gymnastics **competitions**. She won three straight world titles and four US national **championships**. As of 2016, Simone had won 14 world **medals**. And, she hadn't lost an all-around competition since 2013.

In 2014, Simone won gold at the FIG World Championships in China.

In 2013, Simone traveled to Belgium. She won the all-around competition at the FIG World Championships.

In 2015, the FIG World Championships were in Scotland. Simon won another gold medal.

TEAM TRAINING

In July 2016, Simone was chosen to be part of the US women's Olympic gymnastics team. Her teammates were Gabby Douglas, Laurie Hernandez, Madison Kocian, and Aly Raisman. They spent the next few months training together with Team USA **coach** Martha Karolyi.

DID YOU KNOW?
Simone lives an hour away from coach Martha's training center.

Coach Martha has participated in 11 Olympics!

Coach Martha's training center is in Huntsville, Texas. The national team trains there once a month.

RIO OLYMPICS

Olympic **competition** began on August 3, 2016, in Rio de Janeiro, Brazil. All five US team members **performed** well. They earned a team score of 184.897. But, Simone was the star! Her scores helped the team earn a gold **medal**.

After the team won, they called themselves the Final Five. They chose the name to honor **coach** Martha. This is the last time Martha will coach the US Olympic team.

When the Final Five won the gold, it was the first time the US women won the team competition in two straight Olympics.

OLYMPIC STAR

Two days later, Simone was in the individual all-around **competition**. She scored a 15.933 on her floor routine. This was the highest score of the night. Simone won her second gold **medal** by more than two points!

DID YOU KNOW ?
In an all-around competition, gymnasts perform in all events. For women, these are balance beam, floor exercise, uneven bars, and vault.

Simone is four feet nine inches (1.5 m) tall! Her small size allows her to easily perform many flips and tumbles.

Simone continued her **dominance** at the Olympics. She won a gold **medal** in the vault. Then, Simone earned a bronze medal on the balance beam. During her last event, she flipped her way to a gold medal on her floor exercise.

Simone was chosen to carry the American flag at the Olympics closing ceremony.

OUTSIDE THE GYM

When Simone isn't training, she spends time with her family. On Sundays, the Biles family attends church.

Simone also represents many products. She has appeared in **advertisements** for many companies.

In 2016, Simone became part of Team Kellogg's. She promoted Kellogg's products alongside other Olympic athletes.

BUZZ

After the 2016 Olympics, Simone will be part of a gymnastics tour. The Olympic team will **perform** in 36 cities around the United States. Then she plans to take a year off from gymnastics.

Fans hope she will take part in the 2020 Olympics in Tokyo, Japan. They are excited to see what's next for Simone Biles!

In 2016, the Final Five visited the Empire State Building. This is in New York City, New York. It is one of the tallest buildings in the United States.

GLOSSARY

advertisement (ad-vuhr-TEYZE-muhnt) a short message in print or on television or radio that helps sell a product.

championship a game, a match, or a race held to find a first-place winner.

coach someone who teaches or trains a person or a group on a certain subject or skill.

competition (kahm-puh-TIH-shuhn) a contest between two or more people or groups. To compete is to take part in a contest between two or more persons or groups.

dominant commanding or controlling all others.

foster home a household in which a child lives for a period of time to be cared for by people who are not his or her parents.

medal an award for success.

perform to do something in front of an audience.

sibling a brother or a sister.

WEBSITES

To learn more about Olympic Biographies, visit **booklinks.abdopublishing.com**.
These links are routinely monitored and updated to provide
the most current information available.

INDEX